TRUE FINANCIAL FREEDOM

How to Honor God with Our Money

BRANDON K MOORE

True Financial Freedom

ISBN (paperback): 978-1-957812-13-7

ISBN (e-book): 978-1-957812-12-0

CONTENTS

1
TRUE WEALTH AND FINANCIAL FREEDOM

"The rich rule over the poor, and the borrower is slave to the lender."

— Proverbs 22:7 (NIV)

Growing up, I never imagined I'd spend so much time thinking about money—especially since it seemed there was never enough of it. Like many people, I used to think that freedom meant having more money or, maybe, hitting a big break that would solve all my problems. But true financial freedom isn't about landing a windfall or even accumulating a fortune. It's about being free from the need to constantly chase after money and being able to use what you have in a way that honors God, serves others, and fulfills the purpose He's set for your life.

Financial freedom is about more than just dollars in the bank. It's about peace. It's having a sense of stability, direction, and the confidence to follow God's calling without being shackled by financial worries. And, most importantly, it's about avoiding the pitfalls that lead us into financial slavery—debt, greed, and the relentless pursuit of wealth for its own sake. I've had to learn this the hard way, but it's one of the most important lessons of my life.

So, let's talk about what true financial freedom looks like, the steps to get there, and how we can build a foundation rooted in God's Word.

What is Financial Freedom?

Financial freedom isn't about having a certain number in the bank or living a luxurious lifestyle. It's about making choices based on purpose, not pressure. You see, true freedom is knowing that God is your provider, not the numbers in your bank account. You're free when you can choose to follow God's calling without the nagging stress of debt or the constant pressure to earn more just to make ends meet.

In Matthew 6:24, Jesus tells us something profound: *"No one can serve two masters... You cannot serve both God and money."* If money is our main focus, it will control our decisions, and we'll end up feeling like slaves to it. But when we let God lead, everything changes. We no longer have to be ruled by the world's definition of wealth; instead, we're free to pursue something more meaningful.

To put it simply, financial freedom means seeing money as a tool, not a treasure. It means controlling your money instead of letting it control you. When money is in its right place, it becomes a resource to fulfill God's purpose, to serve others, and to live a life of joy and peace.

Freedom from Debt: Breaking the Chains

One of the biggest roadblocks to financial freedom is debt. Debt creates chains that tie you to your past decisions, restrict your present, and limit your future. Proverbs 22:7 makes this very clear: *"The rich rule over the poor, and the borrower is slave to the lender."* Debt isn't just about owing money; it's about being locked into obligations that can limit your ability to act freely and follow God's calling.

I remember when my wife and I were just starting out, every month was a balancing act. We were stretched thin, making payments on loans, a car, and credit cards. It was stressful. But as I learned to manage our money according to God's principles, I realized that debt wasn't just a financial issue—it was a mindset. Debt makes us slaves to other people's priorities, and it distracts us from our own purpose.

The journey to freedom started with a decision to live within our means, even if that meant making sacrifices. We had to learn the discipline of saying "no" to certain things, knowing it would pay off later. Romans 13:8 advises us to *"keep out of debt altogether, except that perpetual debt of love."* This doesn't mean it's always wrong to borrow money, but it means we shouldn't let debt become a habit or a way of life. When you're weighed down by debt, it's hard to experience the freedom and peace God desires for you.

Freedom from the Love of Money

Let's get one thing clear: Money itself isn't the problem. It's the *love* of money that gets us into trouble. 1 Timothy 6:10 is often misquoted, but it actually says, *"For the love of money is a root of all kinds of evil."* When we put money on a pedestal, it distorts our values, and we start making decisions that aren't aligned with God's will.

One of the biggest traps in our culture today is the idea that having more money equals more happiness. But Jesus had a different perspective. He taught us to *"seek first His kingdom and His righteousness, and all these things will be given to you as well"* (Matthew 6:33). When we focus on God's purpose for our lives, He provides for our needs.

So, what does freedom from the love of money look like? It's about recognizing that God is our provider and that He knows what we need. It's about letting go of the need to constantly acquire more and learning to be content with what we have. True wealth isn't measured by the size of your bank account; it's measured by the peace, purpose, and joy that come from trusting in God's provision.

Freedom from Financial Pressure

Financial pressure is one of the most common stressors in life, and it can be overwhelming. When you're constantly worried about money, every decision feels like life or death, and it's hard to focus on anything else. But Jesus speaks directly to this in Matthew 6:25-34, telling us not to worry about what we'll eat, drink, or wear. God knows what we need, and He promises to provide for us.

Early in my career, I was constantly under financial pressure. I thought that if I just worked a little harder, earned a little more, or closed a few more deals, things would finally fall into place. But that kind of thinking never brought me peace; it only led to more stress. Philippians 4:6-7 became my lifeline: *"Do not be anxious about anything, but in every situation, by prayer and petition, with thanksgiving, present your requests to God."*

Real financial freedom comes from trusting God with our needs. When we align our lives with His priorities and follow His principles, we can let go of the constant pressure to control everything. Instead, we can live with a sense of peace and security, knowing that God is in control.

Four Steps to Financial Freedom

If you're ready to pursue financial freedom, here are four essential steps to guide you on your journey. Each one requires faith, discipline, and a willingness to trust God with every aspect of your financial life.

1. Break Free from the Spirit of Poverty

Poverty isn't just about a lack of money; it's a mindset. It's the belief that you'll never have enough and that scarcity is your reality. But Luke 4:18 tells us that Jesus came to *"proclaim good news to the poor... to set the oppressed free."* Breaking free from a poverty mindset means believing in God's abundance and understanding that He wants to bless you so you can be a blessing to others.

2. Cultivate Faith in God

Faith is the foundation of financial freedom. A proper attitude toward God recognizes Him as our ultimate provider. In Joshua 1:8, we're reminded to *"meditate on God's word"* to be "prosperous and successful." When we trust God's promises over our financial fears, we experience true freedom. Trusting God with our finances means we don't have to scramble to provide for ourselves—He's already got us covered.

3. Develop a Right Attitude Toward Yourself

Financial freedom requires personal responsibility. Proverbs 27:23 tells us to *"know well the condition of your flocks, and give attention to your herds."* This means understanding your financial situation, creating a budget, and being intentional with your resources. Financial freedom doesn't happen by accident; it's the result of careful planning, wise decisions, and the self-discipline to live within our means.

4. Change Your Financial Behavior

True financial freedom comes when we transform how we handle money. James 1:22 reminds us to be doers of the Word, not just hearers. That means we need to take action—whether it's paying off debt, building a budget, or saving for the future. Aligning our financial practices with God's principles allows us to experience the freedom that comes from obedience and faithfulness.

Financial freedom isn't about having everything you want; it's about having what you need and trusting God for the rest. When you live according to His principles and prioritize His purpose, you'll find peace, stability, and the freedom to pursue what truly matters. Let God lead your financial journey, and you'll see His faithfulness in every area of your life.

Discussion Questions:

1. What does financial freedom mean for you?

2. How committed to your financial freedom are you?

3. What is the biggest barrier to your financial freedom?

4. When you picture your life in financial freedom, what priorities would consume your time?

2
STEWARDSHIP — OWNING NOTHING, MANAGING EVERYTHING

"The earth is the Lord's, and everything in it, the world, and all who live in it."

— Psalm 24:1 (NIV)

When I first started out as a business owner, I wanted to make my mark. I wanted to build something significant, something that could make a difference and support my family. But, if I'm honest, there was a lot of pride in it, too. I saw success as something I could own, a measure of my achievements. It took me years to realize that everything I thought was mine—my business, my money, my time—wasn't mine at all. It was God's.

Understanding stewardship starts with that foundational truth: God owns everything. Our job is to manage what He's entrusted to us. This perspective changes everything about how we handle money, work, and even our dreams. As 1 Chronicles 29:11-12 reminds us, *"Yours, O Lord, is the greatness, the power, the glory, the victory, and the majesty… everything in the heavens and on earth is yours."*

What Does it Mean to be a Steward?

The word "stewardship" may sound old-fashioned, but it's as relevant today as ever. A steward is someone who manages another's property, looking after it responsibly and wisely. In modern terms, it's like being an asset manager—but God's assets. God is the ultimate owner, and our role is to handle His resources as He would want.

In simple terms, stewardship means taking good care of what God has given us. This includes our finances, but also our time, our talents, and even our relationships. Stewardship is about realizing that everything we have is a gift from God and should be used to honor Him and fulfill His purposes. Deuteronomy 8:17-18 warns us not to take credit for our own success, saying, *"Remember the Lord your God, for it is he who gives you the ability to produce wealth."*

Recognizing God's Ownership

The idea that "God owns everything" is not just a nice thought; it's a reality that should shape our actions. Psalm 50:10-12 says, *"For every animal of the forest is mine, and the cattle on a thousand hills… the world is mine, and all that is in it."* This means that every dollar in our bank account and every resource we hold is ultimately His. We are simply caretakers, called to manage these resources with integrity.

When you recognize God's ownership, it changes how you spend, save, and give. Suddenly, money becomes a tool for God's work, not a measure of personal success. Every decision becomes a matter of asking, "How would God want me to use His resources in this situation?"

Practical Stewardship: Living in Trust

If God is the owner, then our job is to manage. This concept of stewardship challenges us to be intentional about how we handle everything from our finances to our possessions. Here are a few ways to start:

1. **Budget with Purpose** – When we budget, we're making a plan to manage God's resources responsibly. A budget isn't just about paying bills; it's about allocating funds in a way that honors Him. Proverbs 27:23 reminds us, *"Be sure you know the condition of your flocks, give careful attention to your herds."* This verse speaks to the importance of knowing where our resources are going and why.

2. **Save with Discipline** – Saving isn't about hoarding; it's about preparing for the future. Proverbs 21:20 says, *"The wise store up choice food and olive oil, but fools gulp theirs down."* Saving allows us to be prepared for unexpected expenses and opportunities to give. By setting aside a portion of what God has given, we're acting as wise stewards of His gifts.

3. **Give with Generosity** – Giving is one of the most powerful ways to show that we trust God's provision. When we give, we acknowledge that He is our source. The Bible encourages us to give joyfully, not out of obligation but as an act of worship. 2 Corinthians 9:7 says, *"Each of you should give what you have decided in your heart to give, not reluctantly or under compulsion, for God loves a cheerful giver."*

Stewardship is About Trust

Stewardship isn't about following a set of rules; it's about trust. When we view our possessions as God's, we trust Him to provide for our needs and guide our financial decisions. One of the greatest promises in Scripture is that God will meet our needs when we trust Him. Jesus reassures us in Matthew 6:33, *"Seek first his kingdom and his righteousness, and all these things will be given to you as well."*

It's not always easy to trust God with our finances. I've had seasons where the future looked uncertain, and it was tempting to hold onto every dollar. But God has shown me time and again that when I let go, He provides in ways I couldn't have imagined.

Living as a Trustee

Being a steward also means understanding that we're trustees. Imagine that God has given you a trust account filled with resources to manage for His kingdom. Every dollar, every hour, and every opportunity is part of that trust. When we use these resources wisely, we honor God.

Jesus teaches this principle in the Parable of the Talents (Matthew 25:14-30). Each servant was given resources to manage, and their master expected them to use those resources well. The one who buried his talent out of fear lost what he had, while the faithful servants who used their talents wisely were rewarded. God entrusts us with resources, expecting us to use them for His glory, not to bury them out of fear or mismanagement.

Avoiding Mismanagement: Common Pitfalls

We all make mistakes, but there are a few key pitfalls to watch out for when managing God's resources:

1. **Impulse Buying** – Buying on impulse often leads to regret. It's easy to justify purchases, but if they don't align with God's purpose, we're not stewarding well. Before making a big purchase, pause and pray about it.

2. **Neglecting Maintenance** – Stewardship includes caring for what we already have. Proverbs 24:30-34 speaks to this when it says, "I went past the field of a sluggard… thorns had come up everywhere, the ground was covered with weeds, and the stone wall was in ruins." When we neglect what we own, we're not honoring the resources God has given us.

3. **Living Beyond Our Means** – Financial stress often comes from spending more than we earn. Stewardship means living within our means and avoiding debt. Romans 13:8 says, *"Let no debt remain outstanding, except the continuing debt to love one another."* When we avoid unnecessary debt, we free ourselves to give and serve without financial burdens.

The Battle Against Greed

One of the biggest enemies of stewardship is greed. Colossians 3:5 warns us to *"put to death, therefore, whatever belongs to your earthly nature... greed, which is idolatry."* Greed is the opposite of stewardship; it's the desire to have more for the sake of having more. It can lead us to prioritize wealth over God's purpose, turning money into an idol.

Jesus warns us to be on guard against greed in Luke 12:15, saying, *"Watch out! Be on your guard against all kinds of greed; life does not consist in an abundance of possessions."* A steward's job isn't to amass wealth but to manage resources wisely, giving generously and using money to further God's work.

A Prayer of Relinquishment

To truly live as stewards, we must relinquish ownership and acknowledge God's sovereignty. Here's a prayer of relinquishment:

Dear Lord, I acknowledge that everything I have belongs to You. I am only a steward, entrusted to manage Your resources wisely. Help me to honor You with my finances, my time, and my talents. May my life reflect Your generosity, and may I serve others with the blessings You've given. Amen.

Stewardship isn't just a principle; it's a lifestyle rooted in trust, discipline, and generosity. When we live as stewards, we find freedom from financial stress, knowing that God is the true owner and provider of all we have. This journey isn't always easy, but it's one of the most rewarding ways we can honor God with our lives.

Discussion Questions:

1. How does a stewardship mindset differ than a consumption mindset?

2. When have you been trusted with someone else's things and then been given your own? What did you learn from that experience?

3. What do you do to avoid impulse buying? What things lend themselves to impulse buying?

4. Trusting God with our finances is tough. What steps can you take to begin that process?

3

THE ART OF CONTENTMENT

"But godliness with contentment is great gain. For we brought nothing into the world, and we can take nothing out of it. But if we have food and clothing, we will be content with that."

— 1 Timothy 6:6-8 (NIV)

In a world driven by ambition, contentment isn't just rare—it's countercultural. For most of my life, I thought contentment meant settling, as if it were some consolation prize. But over time, I realized contentment isn't about giving up on dreams or ambition. It's about being at peace with what you have, where you are, and trusting that God knows what's best for you. Contentment is the foundation for real joy and financial freedom.

I used to think that happiness was just one more paycheck away, that I'd finally be content if I could just upgrade this or achieve that. But here's the truth: contentment has nothing to do with what you have and everything to do with how you see your life. Jesus tells us in Luke 12:15, *"A man's life does not consist in the abundance of his possessions."* True contentment is about finding joy and satisfaction in God's provision right now, not in the endless chase for more.

Contentment is an Attitude

Contentment isn't about reaching a certain financial status; it's an attitude. It's a choice to live gratefully, even when things don't look perfect. Life is a journey, and God wants us to enjoy each step of it—not just the finish line. If you think your happiness is waiting for you in some distant "better" version of your life, you'll spend your days chasing the wind.

I love how the Apostle Paul puts it in Philippians 4:11-13: *"I have learned to be content whatever the circumstances. I know what it is to be in need, and I know what it is to have plenty. I have learned the secret of being content in any and every situation... I can do all this through him who gives me strength."* Paul didn't find contentment because he had everything he wanted. He found it because he trusted that Jesus was enough, no matter what.

The Difference Between Contentment and Complacency

Here's where we often get tripped up: contentment doesn't mean complacency. Contentment is spiritual rest, a peaceful acceptance of God's provision. Complacency, on the other hand, is giving up on growth. Complacency says, "This is as good as it gets," while contentment says, "This is good because God is in control." We're called to grow and strive in our gifts, but we're also called to rest in what God has provided and not live in constant dissatisfaction.

Hebrews 13:5 reminds us, *"Keep your lives free from the love of money and be content with what you have, because God has said, 'Never will I leave you; never will I forsake you.'"* When we're content, we're living out the belief that God's presence and provision are enough. That's not complacency—that's faith.

Practical Steps to Embrace Contentment

The art of contentment doesn't come naturally to most of us. It's something we have to practice. Here are a few steps that have helped me embrace contentment along the way:

1. **Reduce Living Expenses Below Income**

   Living within our means is foundational to contentment. Proverbs 21:20 tells us, *"The wise store up choice food and olive oil, but fools gulp theirs down."* Instead of always trying to level up, try reducing expenses to create margin. This financial breathing room can bring a sense of freedom that outshines any temporary high from a new purchase.

2. **Value What You Have**

   Start focusing on the blessings you already have rather than what you wish you had. I Thessalonians 5:18 says, *"Give thanks in all circumstances."* Cultivating gratitude shifts our mindset from scarcity to abundance, helping us see the good right in front of us.

3. **Express Appreciation**

   Make it a habit to thank God daily for the things we often take for granted—health, relationships, and even challenges that teach us resilience. Being intentional about gratitude for the basics grounds us, making it easier to feel content.

4. **Find Joy in Stewardship**

   There's something fulfilling about caring for what God has given us. When we take good care of our belongings, we're acknowledging that they are blessings, not entitlements. Luke 16:10-12 puts it this way: *"Whoever can be trusted with very little can also be trusted with much... And if you have not been trustworthy with someone else's property, who will give you property of your own?"*

Contentment doesn't mean we stop dreaming or pursuing new goals, but it does mean we learn to find peace in the journey.

Discovering the Real Value of Money

To build a healthy relationship with money, it's crucial to understand its true value. Money is a tool, nothing more. It won't bring contentment, happiness, or identity. Our value comes from God, not our bank account. As 2 Corinthians 6:10 says, *"...having nothing, and yet possessing everything."* That's the paradox of faith: we may lack material wealth, but in Christ, we have everything we need.

Learning the Value of Work

Work is essential not just to earn money but to fulfill God's command. Genesis 2:15 tells us, *"The Lord God took the man and put him in the Garden of Eden to work it and take care of it."* Work isn't a curse—it's a calling. It provides not only for our physical needs but also gives us a sense of purpose and an opportunity to represent God.

As Christians, we're encouraged to give our best in whatever we do. Colossians 3:23-24 instructs us, *"Whatever you do, work at it with all your heart, as working for the Lord, not for human masters, since you know that you will receive an inheritance from the Lord as a reward."* When we see our work as a service to God, it changes how we approach it.

Training Our Kids in Financial Responsibility

One of the best gifts we can give to the next generation is a healthy understanding of money. Proverbs 22:6 says, *"Train up a child in the way he should go, and when he is old he will not depart from it."* Kids need to learn that money doesn't grow on trees; it's earned through hard work and wise decisions. Teaching them to manage money with gratitude and responsibility sets them up for a life of freedom, not enslavement to debt.

Earning More with Integrity

We all want to improve our circumstances, and there's nothing wrong with that. The Bible doesn't discourage hard work or ambition; it simply cautions us to keep our priorities in check. If you want to earn more, make sure it aligns with God's principles. Increase your value through honest work, skill-building, and dedication, as advised in Proverbs 22:29, *"Do you see someone skilled in their work? They will serve before kings; they will not serve before officials of low rank."*

Here are a few ways to increase your earning capacity without compromising your values:

1. **Become Indispensable**

   Aim to be excellent in your field. As you grow in skill and expertise, your value to others naturally increases. Matthew 25:23 reminds us that faithful service is rewarded, saying, *"Well done, good and faithful servant!"*

2. **Develop a Proprietary Instinct**

   Don't just work for a paycheck; invest yourself in the success of your work or business. Treat it as if it were your own. This mindset not only enhances your performance but also attracts opportunities.

3. **Learn from Others**

   Surround yourself with people who are successful in the areas where you want to grow. Proverbs 13:20 says, *"Walk with the wise and become wise, for a companion of fools suffers harm."* Seek mentors and learn from their successes and mistakes.

4. **Keep Your Heart in Check**

   Money is a tool, not a goal. Keep your focus on God, who is the true provider of all we have. Mark 10:43-44 emphasizes servanthood as greatness in God's Kingdom: *"Whoever wants to become great among you must be your servant."* We grow in God's favor when we prioritize service over personal gain.

Finding Spiritual Benefits in Money

Money can do more than just meet our needs; it can also serve spiritual purposes. When managed well, it can:

1. **Develop Trustworthiness**

   Luke 16:11 says, *"If you have not been trustworthy in handling worldly wealth, who will trust you with true riches?"* Our approach to money is a reflection of our spiritual integrity. When we're faithful with finances, we're building the character God desires.

2. **Meet Daily Needs**

   God uses money to meet our practical needs, reminding us of His faithfulness. Matthew 6:11, *"Give us today our daily bread,"* emphasizes that our provision comes from God.

3. **Support Others Generously**

   Money allows us to give back and support others. Ephesians 4:28 encourages us to work so that we *"may have something to share with those in need."* Generosity is one of the most tangible ways we can demonstrate God's love.

4. **Lay Up Treasure in Heaven**

   Jesus tells us in Matthew 6:19-21 not to store up treasures on earth, but to lay up treasures in heaven. Money invested in God's Kingdom—through giving, helping others, and serving—has eternal value.

Contentment isn't about lowering your expectations or giving up on success. It's about living with a heart rooted in gratitude and trusting that God's provision is enough. As we grow in contentment, we experience the true joy and freedom that come from knowing our worth isn't tied to a paycheck or possessions. In a world that constantly tells us to want more, may we remember that we are already rich in Christ.

Discussion Questions:

1. How do you express contentment to your boss, family, friends?

2. What does earning with integrity mean to you?

3. What is the value of work? How does it satisfy our needs for purpose, significance?

4. How does the Kingdom of God benefit from our work? How do you connect what you do to your purpose?

4

THE DEBT TRAP — BREAKING FREE FROM FINANCIAL BONDAGE

"The rich rule over the poor, and the borrower is slave to the lender."

— Proverbs 22:7 (NIV)

Debt can be a slippery slope. One moment, it feels like an opportunity to get ahead, but before long, it can feel like a chain holding you down. I've been there, and I know how easy it is to fall into the trap. Our culture tells us that debt is normal—even that it's necessary for success. But as Christians, we're called to live differently. Debt isn't just a financial burden; it's a spiritual one. It binds us, limits our freedom, and hinders our ability to serve God fully.

When you're buried under debt, it's hard to experience true financial freedom. Every paycheck feels like it's already spent, and there's constant pressure to earn more just to keep up with payments. That's not the life God wants for us. Proverbs 22:7 reminds us that debt makes us a servant to someone else's agenda. True freedom comes when we're able to focus on God's plans, not on monthly payments.

Borrowing: A Modern-Day Pitfall

Debt has become a way of life in modern society. We're surrounded by offers for "easy payments" and "instant credit," but every dollar we borrow comes with strings attached. These "easy" loans might seem like a quick solution, but they often end up costing us much more in the long run. Proverbs 14:12 says, *"There is a way that appears to be right, but in the end it leads to death."* Borrowing might seem like the right path at the moment, but it often leads to a life burdened with stress, missed opportunities, and financial strain.

The problem is, debt can accumulate faster than we realize. It starts small—maybe a credit card to cover a few purchases—but it can snowball. A study showed that many families overspend by as little as $100 each month, yet that small overspend, with interest, can grow to tens of thousands in debt over a few years to fall into this cycle, and getting out can feel impossible. But the good news is, with God's help, there is a way out.

Recognizing the Signs of Debt Trouble

The first step to escaping the debt trap is to recognize the signs. Debt is often a symptom of deeper issues—impulse spending, a lack of discipline, or even using money to fill an emotional void. If you're using one credit card to pay another, relying on loans to cover everyday expenses, or struggling to pay the minimum amount due each month, it's time to make a change.

Proverbs 13:15 warns, *"The way of transgressors is hard."* Debt makes life hard, not because God is punishing us, but because it leads us away from the peace and freedom He wants for us. It's time to take a hard look at our spending habits, be honest with ourselves, and commit to a new path.

Eight Consequences of Debt

To really grasp the impact of debt, we need to understand what it costs us, not just financially, but spiritually and emotionally as well. Here are eight consequences of living in debt:

1. **It Consumes Resources** – Debt eats away at our resources through interest payments, reducing what we have available for God's work, our family, and our future.

2. **It Hinders Generosity** – When debt takes a significant portion of our income, it limits our ability to give and support causes that matter. Luke 6:38 reminds us, *"Give, and it will be given to you."* Debt limits our ability to live out that calling.

3. **It Interferes with God's Provision** – God has promised to meet our needs, but debt can become a crutch that keeps us from relying on Him fully. Philippians 4:19 says, *"And my God will meet all your needs according to the riches of his glory in Christ Jesus."* When we trust in debt rather than in God, we miss out on experiencing His provision.

4. **It Reduces Flexibility** – Debt locks us into obligations, limiting our ability to respond to God's calling when He opens new doors.

5. **It Harms Relationships** – Financial stress is a leading cause of marital problems and can create tension with family and friends.

6. **It Leads to Impulse Spending** – Debt fosters a mentality of "buy now, pay later," which often leads to purchases we don't need and can't afford.

7. **It Presumes on the Future** – Taking on debt assumes that tomorrow will bring increased income, but James 4:13-14 reminds us, *"You do not even know what will happen tomorrow."*

8. **It Diminishes God's Reputation** – As Christians, our financial stewardship reflects God's provision. Debt can give the impression that we need more than He provides.

Steps to Break Free from Debt

If you're ready to break free from debt, the journey starts with a commitment to change. Here's a roadmap that can help you take practical, faith-based steps toward financial freedom.

1. Pray and Seek God's Guidance

Start by asking God to help you get out of debt and give you the strength to follow through. Proverbs 3:5-6 encourages us, *"Trust in the Lord with all your heart and lean not on your own understanding; in all your ways submit to him, and he will make your paths straight."* Financial freedom isn't just about numbers; it's about relying on God's wisdom.

2. Commit to No New Debt

One of the most important steps is to stop adding new debt. This might mean sacrificing or delaying some purchases, but it's worth it. Credit cards and loans should no longer be a "safety net." If you're serious about financial freedom, put the cards away and consider a cash-only approach for a while. Matthew 6:24 reminds us, *"No one can serve two masters... You cannot serve both God and money."*

3. Face the Reality of Your Situation

Debt can be overwhelming, and it's tempting to avoid looking at the full picture. But freedom starts with honesty. Make a list of all your debts, including balances, interest rates, and minimum payments. Proverbs 27:23 says, *"Be sure you know the condition of your flocks, give careful attention to your herds."* Knowing exactly what you owe is the first step toward paying it off.

4. Create a Debt Repayment Plan

Once you have a clear picture of your debts, develop a plan. The "snowball" method is a popular strategy: start by paying off your smallest debt first, then roll that payment into the next smallest debt, creating momentum as each debt is cleared. Alternatively, you can tackle the debt with the highest interest rate first. Choose a strategy that keeps you motivated.

5. Live Below Your Means

To pay off debt faster, you'll need to cut back on spending and direct those savings toward debt. Proverbs 21:5 reminds us, *"The plans of the diligent lead to profit."* By living below your means, you'll free up money to eliminate debt more quickly and build a buffer for the future.

6. Seek Additional Income

If possible, look for ways to increase your income. Whether it's a side job, freelancing, or selling unneeded items, every extra dollar can go toward reducing debt. And remember to ask God for creativity in finding these opportunities—He may open doors you hadn't considered.

7. Trust God's Provision

It can be challenging to resist the urge to borrow when unexpected expenses arise. But remember, God has promised to provide. Matthew 6:33 reassures us, *"But seek first his kingdom and his righteousness, and all these things will be given to you as well."* Trust in His timing and provision as you work to free yourself from debt.

8. Rejoice in Small Victories

Debt reduction is a marathon, not a sprint. Celebrate each small victory—every debt you pay off, every month you stay within budget, every moment you trust God instead of relying on debt. Philippians 4:4 encourages us, *"Rejoice in the Lord always. I will say it again: Rejoice!"* These milestones are reminders of God's faithfulness.

Living Debt-Free: A Life of Freedom and Generosity

Imagine the freedom of living debt-free. When you're no longer burdened by debt, you have more resources to bless others, to support God's work, and to respond to His call with an open heart. Debt limits our ability to live generously, but when those chains are broken, the possibilities are endless.

Debt isn't just a financial problem; it's a spiritual one. It can steal your peace, limit your freedom, and hinder your ability to serve. But by following God's principles and trusting in His provision, you can break free from the debt trap and experience the abundant life He promises. Remember, financial freedom isn't about never borrowing again; it's about learning to trust God as your provider and finding contentment in His provision.

Discussion Questions:

1. What is your history with debt? Families history with debt?

2. How is debt used as a tool? What are some positive uses of debt?

3. How is debt used as a trap? When have you used debt to finance something you regretted?

4. What does it feel like to pay off something, like a car, house, or large purchase? What does it feel like to pay for a large purchase with cash?

5
THE GRACE OF GIVING

"Give, and it will be given to you. A good measure, pressed down, shaken together and running over, will be poured into your lap. For with the measure you use, it will be measured to you."

— Luke 6:38 (NIV)

If there's one principle I've learned in my journey with money, it's this: God's math is different from ours. He doesn't count dollars in the same way we do. In our world, it seems like giving means having less. But in God's Kingdom, giving is a gateway to abundance. Generosity unlocks blessings, joy, and even a sense of purpose we can't find in self-centered living.

When I was young, I thought the idea of "giving" meant just dropping some money in the offering plate or helping out when it felt convenient. But as I grew in faith, I realized that giving is so much more than that—it's a lifestyle, a reflection of trust in God, and a doorway to experiencing His blessings. The Bible teaches us that giving is not just a duty but a "grace" (2 Corinthians 8:7), a privilege and joy that God invites us into.

Giving as a Reflection of Faith

One of the core questions every Christian has to answer is, "Do I trust God to meet my needs?" When we give, we're declaring, "Yes, God, I trust You." Jesus tells us in Matthew 6:21, *"For where your treasure is, there your heart will be also."* Where we choose to put our money reveals where we're placing our faith and where our heart truly lies.

I remember a time early in my career when finances were tight. Every dollar felt precious, and the thought of giving felt risky. But one night, while praying over my finances, I felt God asking me to give more than I thought I could afford. It felt counterintuitive. Yet, when I took that step of faith, God opened doors I couldn't have imagined—opportunities, relationships, and even financial blessings that confirmed His faithfulness. The experience taught me that when we put God first, He always provides.

The Blessing of Generosity

Giving isn't just about transferring money; it's a tangible act of worship. Proverbs 11:24-25 says, *"One person gives freely, yet gains even more; another withholds unduly, but comes to poverty. A generous person will prosper; whoever refreshes others will be refreshed."* There's a joy and freedom in giving that can't be found anywhere else. When we bless others, we find ourselves refreshed, encouraged, and connected to God's heart.

This doesn't mean that giving should be a way to get something back. Instead, giving invites us into a cycle of blessing that honors God's promise to supply our needs. Generosity, when done with a heart to serve and honor God, allows us to experience His provision in new ways.

Why Giving is a Grace

In 2 Corinthians 8:7, Paul calls giving a "grace." Grace, by definition, is a gift we don't earn, and in the same way, giving is a privilege that goes beyond obligation. When we view giving as a grace, it shifts our mindset from "How much do I have to give?" to "How much do I get to give?" God invites us into His work through our giving, and it's a blessing to be part of something bigger than ourselves.

Giving Out of Love, Not Obligation

The Bible teaches us to give cheerfully, not reluctantly or out of obligation. 2 Corinthians 9:7 reminds us, *"Each of you should give what you have decided in your heart to give, not reluctantly or under compulsion, for God loves a cheerful giver."* When we give out of love, our heart aligns with God's purposes. We're not just "donating" to a cause; we're investing in God's Kingdom with joy and expectancy.

Different Forms of Giving

Giving can look different for each of us. God's call to generosity isn't limited to financial gifts—it includes our time, skills, and resources. Here are a few ways to practice this grace of giving:

1. Tithing: Honoring God with the Firstfruits

Tithing—giving the first 10% of our income—is a biblical principle that demonstrates our trust in God as our provider. Malachi 3:10 tells us, *"Bring the whole tithe into the storehouse, that there may be food in my house. Test me in this, says the Lord Almighty, and see if I will not throw open the floodgates of heaven and pour out so much blessing that there will not be room enough to store it."* God invites us to test His faithfulness through tithing, and He promises blessings in return.

Tithing has taught me that God can do more with 90% of my income than I can with 100%. By prioritizing God with the first portion, I've found that He stretches what remains in ways that never cease to amaze me.

2. Giving to Those in Need

Beyond the tithe, the Bible encourages us to give to those in need. In Proverbs 19:17, it says, *"Whoever is kind to the poor lends to the Lord, and he will reward them for what they have done."* When we give to those less fortunate, we're extending God's love and compassion. Every act of kindness—whether it's a meal, a coat, or a helping hand—carries the fragrance of Christ and reflects His heart for the vulnerable.

3. Supporting Ministry and Missions

Giving to support ministry, missions, or your local church allows you to participate in the spread of the Gospel. Paul speaks about the generosity of the Macedonian church in 2 Corinthians 8, noting that they gave even beyond their means to support the work of the Kingdom. Supporting ministry enables the message of Christ to reach places we may never go, impacting lives for eternity.

Developing a Heart of Generosity

Generosity doesn't come naturally for most of us; it's a practice we cultivate over time. Here are a few steps to help develop a generous heart:

1. Start Small and Grow Your Giving

If giving feels challenging, start with a small amount. The widow in Mark 12:41-44 gave only two small coins, yet Jesus said she gave more than all the others because she gave out of her poverty. God sees our hearts, not the amount. Start with what you can give joyfully and grow from there. As your faith and trust in God deepen, you'll find it easier to give more.

2. Make Giving a Priority

Giving should be a priority, not an afterthought. One way to ensure this is to budget for it. Proverbs 3:9 encourages us, *"Honor the Lord with your wealth, with the firstfruits of all your crops."* By setting aside a portion of your income for giving, you'll be able to give consistently and intentionally.

3. Practice Sacrificial Giving

True generosity often requires sacrifice. In 1 Kings 17, the widow at Zarephath gave her last bit of food to the prophet Elijah, trusting God to provide, and He did—her flour and oil never ran out. Sacrificial giving doesn't mean putting yourself in a position of need, but it does mean trusting God with your security. When we give beyond what feels "safe," we invite God's provision in powerful ways.

4. Give in Secret

Jesus taught us in Matthew 6:3-4 to give in secret, without seeking recognition. He said, *"But when you give to the needy, do not let your left hand know what your right hand is doing, so that your giving may be in secret. Then your Father, who sees what is done in secret, will reward you."* Giving in secret guards our hearts against pride and allows us to experience the quiet joy of knowing that God sees and honors our gifts.

The Rewards of Giving

God doesn't promise us wealth or an easy life in return for our giving, but He does promise blessings that go beyond material wealth. Here are some of the rewards of a generous life:

1. Spiritual Growth

Giving draws us closer to God and strengthens our faith. As we trust Him with our finances, we grow in our dependence on Him. Luke 6:38 reminds us, *"For with the measure you use, it will be measured to you."* Generosity builds our faith muscles, teaching us to rely on God's provision.

2. Joy and Fulfillment

There's a unique joy that comes from giving. Acts 20:35 quotes Jesus as saying, *"It is more blessed to give than to receive."* When we give, we experience a deep sense of fulfillment that comes from knowing we've made a difference in someone's life.

3. Eternal Impact

Our gifts can make an eternal impact. When we support ministry, missions, or help someone in need, we're storing up treasures in heaven, as Jesus instructed in Matthew 6:20. This kind of investment doesn't lose value; it multiplies in ways we may never see until eternity.

Giving isn't just a financial decision; it's a spiritual one. It's a declaration that we trust God, that we're committed to His Kingdom, and that we're willing to let go of earthly treasures for eternal ones. When you embrace the grace of giving, you'll find that God's blessings overflow in ways you never expected. Whether you're giving time, talents, or finances, remember that every act of generosity is a reflection of God's love—and that's the greatest investment you can make.

Discussion Questions:

1. How does giving affect your life? How does it impact the Kingdom of God?

2. How can giving impact your community? Your family?

3. When do you decide to give? After all the bills are paid or before? Why does it matter?

4. If you were given $1 million, what would you do with it? What amount would you give away? To whom?

6
BUDGETING – BUILDING A FINANCIAL FOUNDATION

"Any enterprise is built by wise planning, becomes strong through common sense, and profits wonderfully by keeping abreast of the facts."

— Proverbs 24:3-4 (TLB)

When I first started budgeting, I viewed it as a restriction—a set of limits to keep me from enjoying life's pleasures. I thought a budget was something you only needed if you were short on money. But over time, I learned that budgeting isn't about limits; it's about freedom. It's a tool that gives you control, allowing you to prioritize your goals and values rather than letting money dictate your choices. Budgeting is a powerful way to steward God's resources wisely, ensuring you're prepared to fulfill His purposes in every season.

Signals That You Need a Budget

For many of us, the need for a budget becomes clear when we start feeling the strain of financial pressure. Maybe you've been in a situation where payday is still a week away, but your bank account is nearly empty. Or perhaps you're juggling multiple bills, trying to decide which one can wait until next month. If you've experienced any of these signals, it's time to consider a budget:

- Finding it challenging to tithe or give generously
- Letting one or more bills slide into the next month
- Regularly running out of money just before payday
- Not knowing where your money went after each month
- Struggling to save consistently

If any of these sound familiar, a budget can help you regain control. A budget isn't just about numbers; it's about aligning your finances with your values and building a path toward financial peace.

What is a Budget?

At its core, a budget is a plan—a way of telling your money where to go rather than wondering where it went. It's a tool that empowers you to make intentional choices, setting boundaries on spending so you can prioritize what matters most. Proverbs 22:3 reminds us, *"A prudent man foresees the difficulties ahead and prepares for them."* A budget helps us anticipate future needs, avoid financial pitfalls, and create a cushion for unexpected expenses.

Benefits of Budgeting

1. **Improves Awareness** – Without a budget, money often slips through our fingers, and we're left asking, "Where did it all go?" Budgeting provides clarity, showing exactly where your money goes and helping you adjust your habits to align with your goals.

2. **Builds Financial Discipline** – Budgeting trains us to say "no" to impulsive purchases and to focus on our priorities. It's a practice in self-control, which, as Proverbs 25:28 says, is essential: *"A person without self-control is like a city with broken-down walls."*

3. **Supports Generosity** – When you're in control of your finances, it's easier to give freely. Budgeting creates space for generosity, allowing you to give joyfully without sacrificing your financial stability.

4. **Reduces Stress** – There's peace in knowing that every dollar has a purpose. When we budget, we can approach financial challenges with confidence, knowing we're prepared.

Steps to Build a Workable Budget

Creating a budget isn't as complicated as it may seem. With a few simple steps, you can establish a budget that sets you on a path toward financial freedom.

1. Define Your Financial Goals

Before you dive into numbers, take some time to consider your goals. What are you working toward? Maybe it's paying off debt, building an emergency fund, or saving for a big purchase. Having clear goals will motivate you to stick to your budget. Habakkuk 2:2 advises us to *"write the vision and make it plain."* Write down your goals, both short-term and long-term, and review them regularly to stay focused.

2. Track Your Spending History

To create an effective budget, you need to know your spending patterns. Take a look at the last few months' bank statements or receipts to get an idea of where your money goes. This step may reveal areas where you're overspending and help you identify opportunities to save. (See Example 1).

3. Set Realistic Spending Limits

Based on your spending history and financial goals, set limits for each category in your budget. Allocate money to essential expenses like housing, utilities, and groceries, and then prioritize savings, debt repayment, and giving. Luke 14:28 reminds us to *"count the cost,"* emphasizing the importance of planning and setting realistic boundaries for our finances.

4. Plan for the Unexpected

Life is full of surprises, and a budget should account for that. Set aside a portion of your income in an emergency fund for unexpected expenses, like car repairs or medical bills. Proverbs 6:6-8 encourages us to *"take a lesson from the ants… they labor hard all summer, gathering food for the winter."* An emergency fund acts as a financial winter store, providing security and peace of mind.

5. Review and Adjust Monthly

Budgeting isn't a one-time task; it's an ongoing process. At the end of each month, review your budget to see how well you followed it. If you overspent in one category, adjust for the next month. A budget is flexible and should evolve with your financial situation and goals.

Tips for Effective Budgeting

Once you have a budget in place, these tips can help you stay on track and make the most of your money.

Eliminate Consumer Debt

If you're carrying credit card debt or other high-interest loans, make paying them off a priority. Interest payments eat away at your income, limiting your ability to save and give. Proverbs 22:7 warns us, *"The borrower is slave to the lender."* By eliminating debt, you free yourself from financial burdens and open up opportunities to use your money for God's purposes.

Build Savings into Your Budget

Saving shouldn't be an afterthought—it should be a consistent part of your budget. Whether it's for an emergency fund, a future purchase, or retirement, set aside a portion of your income every month. For example, if you know your car insurance premium of $600 is due in six months, set aside $100 each month so you're prepared when the bill arrives. This proactive approach helps you avoid last-minute financial stress.

Records of Cash Expenditures

For one month, try tracking every cash expense, even the small ones. Budget experts recommend this as a way to gain insight into spending habits you might not notice otherwise. This exercise can help you identify areas where you can cut back and save more effectively .

Get Organized

Keeping your records organized is essential for effective budgeting. Store receipts, bank statements, and credit card statements in a designated file, organized by month. At the end of the year, you'll have a complete record of your finances, making it easy to review your progress and make adjustments .

Annual Budget

As your financial situation changes, your budget should, too. At least once a year, review your budget to ensure it still aligns with your goals. Fine-tune spending limits, adjust for new expenses, and celebrate your progress. Budgeting isn't just about restriction—it's about growth and adaptability.

Budgeting for Financial Freedom

The ultimate goal of budgeting is to experience financial freedom. When we're free from debt and confident in our financial plan, we can respond to God's call with open hands. Budgeting is a tool to help us steward His resources well, positioning us to live generously and fulfill His purposes.

Luke 16:10 teaches, *"Whoever can be trusted with very little can also be trusted with much."* A budget is a way of demonstrating our faithfulness with the resources God has given us. As we practice wise management, God entrusts us with more, allowing us to make an even greater impact in His Kingdom.

In the end, budgeting isn't just about numbers—it's about living a life that honors God. By managing our finances wisely, we're not only providing for ourselves and our families; we're creating a foundation to serve, give, and fulfill the unique calling God has placed on each of our lives.

Discussion Questions:

5. How does having a budget affect your peace?

6. Are you a spender or a saver? How does a budget help either type of person?

7. How can budgeting affect your awareness of where your money goes? What apps are available to help you budget?

8. What are barriers that keep you from creating and monitoring your money with a budget? How can you overcome those barriers?

7

BUILDING SALES RESISTANCE - STANDING FIRM AGAINST THE CONSUMER FRENZY

"The simple believe anything, but the prudent give thought to their steps."

— Proverbs 14:15 (NIV)

When it comes to sales and advertising, let's be real: companies spend billions every year trying to convince us that we're just one purchase away from happiness. I remember early in my journey to financial stewardship, I'd find myself captivated by shiny new things—a new phone, a better car, a high-end coffee machine. I'd justify each purchase, convincing myself it was worth it. But here's the thing: stuff didn't make me happier. If anything, it just made me feel like I was always chasing the next thing.

The concept of "sales resistance" is about more than just saying "no" to a salesperson; it's about saying "yes" to wisdom and purpose. Learning to stand firm against the consumer culture isn't about depriving yourself but about protecting your finances, your peace, and your relationship with God.

Understanding the Job of a Salesperson

First, let's start with a reality check. A salesperson isn't there to be your financial counselor; they're there to make a sale. Their job is to convince you that you need what they're selling, and they're trained to make you feel like you're missing out if you don't buy. They paint vivid pictures of how much better your life will be with their product, but it's up to us to look beyond the polished pitch.

Proverbs 23:23 reminds us, *"Get the facts at any price, and hold on tightly to all the good sense you can get."* In a world full of persuasive marketing, we need to be proactive in seeking truth. When we let wisdom guide our spending, we find freedom from impulsive decisions and unnecessary purchases.

Establishing the Accuracy of Sales Pitches

Here's something I've learned over the years: take sales claims with a grain of salt. Every pitch sounds enticing, but not every promise holds up. A salesperson might say, "See how much you'll save!" but what they really mean is, "See how much you'll spend." And when they say, "Easy payments," they mean, "Easy debt."

This discernment is what Proverbs 14:15 calls prudence. We don't just accept what we're told; we dig deeper, weigh the facts, and seek God's guidance before making decisions. When we approach purchases with this mindset, we avoid the regret that often follows impulse buys.

Tips for Strengthening Sales Resistance

Learning to resist the allure of constant consumption isn't easy, but it's essential for building financial freedom. Here are some strategies that have helped me along the way.

1. Treat Every Purchase as Real Money

Credit cards and digital payments can make it easy to forget that we're spending actual money. Whenever you're about to make a purchase, remind yourself that you're using your hard-earned cash. Visualize the hours of work it took to earn that money and consider if the item is truly worth it. Maybe keep a journal of what you spend each day by hand. That way you can see how it adds up.

2. Count the Cost in Hours, Not Dollars

A tip that changed my perspective was calculating the cost of a purchase in terms of hours worked. For example, if you earn $15 an hour and a new gadget costs $300, that's 20 hours of work. This exercise helps you comprehend the true cost and may lead you to pause before making a major purchase.

Jesus encourages us to count the cost in Luke 14:28-30, reminding us that wise decisions require forethought. When we translate costs into hours of work, we gain a fresh perspective on value.

3. Develop a Delayed Action Rule

One of the best ways to build sales resistance is by establishing a "delayed action" rule. Instead of buying something immediately, decide to wait 24 hours or even a week. This waiting period creates space for reflection and prayer, allowing you to consider if the purchase aligns with your values and goals. Hasty decisions are usually the wrong decision.

Hebrews 13:5 reminds us, *"Be content with what you have."* When we wait, we often realize we don't actually need or even want the item. This habit not only saves money but also reinforces a mindset of contentment.

Before Making a Major Purchase, Ask These Questions

Every significant purchase requires wisdom and discernment. Here are a few questions that can help you evaluate whether a purchase is necessary or simply an impulse.

1. **Am I buying out of discontent?**

   Often, we make purchases to fill an emotional void. Advertising preys on this, feeding our desires for things we don't actually need. Recognize when discontent is driving your decision.

2. **Do I really need this right now?**

   Is this purchase an actual necessity, or are you rationalizing it as one? Sometimes, we label wants as needs to justify our spending.

3. **Is there an alternative?**

   Do we have something else already that will meet the need? Can we find it at a garage sale? Can I borrow from someone else for a short period instead of having to buy it myself?

4. **Am I falling for clever marketing?**

   Ads are crafted to create desire, using tactics that appeal to our ego or sense of identity. Be cautious of advertising that appeals to "the lust of the eye" (1 John 2:16).

5. **Is the price fair?**

   Have you comparison-shopped to find the best value? Taking the time to explore options often reveals that the first offer isn't always the best.

6. **Have I investigated the retailer's reputation?**

   Sometimes, paying a bit more for quality and reliable service is worth it, especially if the seller offers warranties or support.

7. **Have I sought the Lord's guidance?**

   When we pray about major purchases, we invite God into our financial decisions. This practice isn't about asking God to give us what we want but seeking His wisdom for what we need.

Proverbs 12:15 tells us, *"The way of fools seems right to them, but the wise listen to advice."* By seeking God's guidance and counsel from trusted friends, we gain a clearer sense of whether a purchase aligns with His plan for us.

Practical Ways to Stretch Your Dollars

While sales resistance is vital, so is smart spending. Here are practical ways to make the most of your money without compromising quality or value.

Food and Groceries

- **Shop with a List**: Impulse buys often happen in the grocery aisle. A list keeps you focused on essentials.
- **Don't Shop Hungry**: This classic tip prevents unnecessary purchases motivated by hunger rather than need.
- **Calculate Unit Prices**: Buying in bulk can save money, but only if you're truly using what you buy.

Utilities and Energy

- **Conserve Energy**: Lowering your thermostat, unplugging devices, and using energy-efficient bulbs can reduce monthly bills.
- **Negotiate with Providers**: Often, utility providers have discounts or promotional rates. A simple call might reduce your bill.

Clothing and Apparel

- **Buy Off-Season**: Purchasing clothes during off-season sales can lead to significant savings.
- **Thrift and Swap**: High-quality clothing can often be found secondhand. Clothing swaps with friends are also a fun, cost-effective way to update your wardrobe.

Embracing the Freedom of Contentment

True sales resistance isn't just about saying "no" to purchases; it's about saying "yes" to contentment. Hebrews 13:5 encourages us to *"be content with what you have, because God has said, 'Never will I leave you; never will I forsake you.'"* When we trust that God provides all we need, we're freed from the endless pursuit of more.

Living with contentment doesn't mean we never buy anything. It means that our purchases come from a place of purpose, not impulse. Instead of chasing after the latest trends or gadgets, we learn to enjoy what we have, recognizing each item as a blessing from God. This shift in perspective leads to lasting joy and financial peace.

The Joy of Financial Independence

By practicing sales resistance and embracing contentment, we step closer to financial independence. This independence isn't about having more money—it's about having the freedom to live according to God's principles and purpose. As we resist the urge to buy without thought, we gain control over our finances, our peace, and our future.

Proverbs 21:20 wisely notes, *"The wise store up choice food and olive oil, but fools gulp theirs down."* Financial independence comes from managing our resources with wisdom and foresight, creating a life where money serves our purpose, not the other way around.

In the end, sales resistance is more than a financial tool; it's a spiritual discipline. As we learn to guard against the constant pull of consumerism, we find freedom in simplicity, joy in contentment, and confidence in God's provision.

Discussion Questions:

1. What does sales resistance mean to you? In the last 30 days, how much could it have saved you?

2. Advertisers are everywhere now. How can you build firewalls into your life to keep them at a distance?

3. What experience do you have with buyer's remorse? Where you buy a product and immediately regret it. What did you learn from that experience?

8
THE POWER OF INVESTING - BUILDING WEALTH WITH PURPOSE

"Be diligent to know the state of your flocks, and attend to your herds; for riches are not forever, nor does a crown endure to all generations."

— Proverbs 27:23-24 (NKJV)

If you're like me, the idea of investing might seem intimidating or even unnecessary. For a long time, I thought investing was just for people with extra money or the wealthy who had reached a place of security. But as I began to understand the biblical principles of stewardship, I realized that investing isn't about amassing wealth for its own sake. It's about preparing for the future, multiplying what God has given us, and building a legacy.

Investing is a powerful tool for Christians. It's about more than growing money; it's about growing influence, impact, and the ability to give. When managed with wisdom, investments can help us honor God by providing for our families, supporting ministries, and creating financial freedom. Let's dive into why and how to invest with a heart that seeks God's purposes above all.

What Is an Investment?

An investment produces both income and appreciation over time. With an outlay of capital or money, the investor expects this asset to increase in value and provide income during its useful life. Investments can be made in real estate, oil and gas mineral interests, partnership interests, promissory notes, stocks, bonds (or their derivatives), small business interest, etc. But for it to be truly an investment it needs both: income and appreciation.

Reasons to Invest

1. To Do Good and Leave a Legacy

Scripture makes it clear that wise financial management is pleasing to God. Luke 19:12-26 tells the Parable of the Ten Minas, where servants are entrusted with resources and rewarded for multiplying them. The servant who hides his mina, fearing loss, is rebuked, while those who invested and increased theirs are praised. This story reveals God's desire for us to make the most of the resources He's entrusted to us.

By investing wisely, we have the opportunity to do good and leave a legacy. Proverbs 13:22 says, *"A good man leaves an inheritance to his children's children."* This inheritance can be financial, but it's also a legacy of wisdom, values, and faith. When we invest thoughtfully, we're not only securing our future but also positioning ourselves to bless future generations.

2. To Provide Financial Freedom and Security

Investing creates financial freedom, a state where we're not bound by financial worries and can fully focus on God's calling. Our goal of investing means the income from our investments will one day pay our living instead of our job. Ecclesiastes 10:19 tells us, *"Money is the answer for everything."* This isn't to say that money solves all problems, but rather that financial resources can address practical needs and empower us to serve God without distraction.

When we invest, we're building a financial foundation that allows us to live freely. We're ensuring that we can support ourselves, our families, and God's work, even in times of economic uncertainty.

3. To Support Ministries and Missions

God's Kingdom work requires resources, and wise investments can help us support it. Paul encourages generosity in 2 Corinthians 9:8, reminding us that God will "abound in every good work" through us when we give generously. By investing and growing our wealth, we position ourselves to fund ministries, support missions, and make a difference in the lives of others.

Getting Started with Investing

Now that we understand the "why" of investing, let's look at the "how." Beginning with a solid foundation is key to successful investing, so here are some essential steps to take before you dive in.

Step 1: Clear Your Debts and Build a Foundation

Before you start investing, it's essential to pay off high-interest debts and establish an emergency fund. Proverbs 22:7 warns, *"The rich rule over the poor, and the borrower is slave to the lender."* Debt can limit your freedom and hinder your financial growth. By paying off debt, you're freeing yourself to invest without the weight of financial obligations.

Once you're debt-free, build an emergency fund to cover three to six months of expenses. This fund provides a buffer against unexpected expenses and helps ensure you won't have to pull from your investments in a crisis.

Step 2: Start Small and Start Early

The beauty of investing lies in the principle of compounding—earning interest on interest. Even small amounts, invested over time, can grow significantly. Ecclesiastes 11:1 says, *"Cast your bread upon the waters, for after many days you will find it again."* Investing with patience and discipline, even if you start small, can yield substantial results over time.

Consider this: if you invest just $100 per month with an annual return of 8%, in 40 years, you could have over $360,000. Small, consistent contributions are powerful when given time to grow. Don't wait to start; even a little now can have a huge impact later. (See Example 2)

Step 3: Choose Your Investments Wisely

When it comes to investing, knowledge is power. Proverbs 24:3-4 tells us, *"By wisdom a house is built, and through understanding it is established."* Understanding your options helps you make informed choices that align with your goals and values. Here are a few types of investments to consider:

1. **Stocks** – Ownership shares in a company. Stocks can grow significantly, but they also carry risk.

2. **Bonds** – Loans to companies or governments, which pay interest over time. Bonds are generally lower risk than stocks but offer lower returns.

3. **Real Estate** – Owning property can provide rental income and appreciate over time. Real estate requires careful research and, ideally, experience in managing property.

4. **Mutual Funds and ETFs** – These funds pool investors' money to buy a diversified portfolio of stocks or bonds, making them a great option for beginners.

5. **Small Businesses, Partnership Interests** – Owning a piece of an income producing business can produce many positive returns. Finding the right business to invest in can be more complicated than finding the right stock, ETF, or mutual fund.

Biblical Principles for Investing

1. Invest with Wisdom and Discernment

Proverbs 21:5 says, *"The plans of the diligent lead to profit as surely as haste leads to poverty."* Successful investing requires diligence, patience, and a willingness to seek wise counsel. Avoid get-rich-quick schemes or investments that promise too-good-to-be-true returns. Instead, focus on solid, long-term strategies that align with your goals.

2. Be Patient and Stay Consistent

Investing is a long-term journey, not a sprint. James 5:7 encourages us to be patient, like a farmer waiting for the crops to grow. Similarly, building wealth through investing takes time and consistency. Avoid the temptation to constantly buy and sell based on market fluctuations. Staying invested and contributing consistently, even during market downturns, is key to long-term growth.

3. Avoid Greed and Embrace Contentment

It's easy to become consumed by the pursuit of wealth, but Scripture warns against this. Ecclesiastes 5:10 reminds us, *"Whoever loves money never has enough; whoever loves wealth is never satisfied with their income."* Guard against greed by focusing on the purpose behind your investments. Remember, wealth is a tool to serve God's kingdom, not an end in itself.

4. Diversify Your Investments

Ecclesiastes 11:2 advises, *"Invest in seven ventures, yes, in eight; you do not know what disaster may come upon the land."* Diversification helps reduce risk, ensuring that if one investment underperforms, others can offset the loss. A diversified portfolio, which includes a mix of stocks, bonds, and other assets, provides stability and long-term growth potential.

Practical Steps for Successful Investing

1. **Set Clear Goals** – Define your investment objectives. Are you saving for retirement, buying a home, or preparing for future giving? Having clear goals keeps you focused and motivated.

2. **Research and Educate Yourself** – The more you understand, the better your decisions will be. Proverbs 4:7 emphasizes the importance of wisdom, urging us to "get understanding." Books, financial podcasts, and courses are excellent resources for learning about investing.

3. **Seek Counsel** – Proverbs 15:22 states, *"Plans fail for lack of counsel, but with many advisers they succeed."* Consider consulting a financial advisor, especially as your portfolio grows. An advisor can help you develop a strategy and provide insights based on your risk tolerance and goals.

The Rewards of Investing Wisely

When we invest wisely, the rewards go beyond financial gain. We experience the peace that comes from knowing we're prepared, the joy of giving from a place of abundance, and the fulfillment of leaving a legacy. Investing empowers us to honor God with our resources, helping us provide for our loved ones, support our church, and bless others.

In Matthew 6:20, Jesus reminds us to *"store up for yourselves treasures in heaven, where moths and vermin do not destroy, and where thieves do not break in and steal."* By investing with a Kingdom mindset, we're building wealth that transcends earthly gains. Wealth managed well becomes a vessel for God's love and provision, reflecting His character and advancing His purposes.

Conclusion: Start Now and Trust God's Provision

The best time to start investing is now. Whether you're beginning with a small amount or a substantial sum, investing is a way to grow what God has given you and prepare for the future. Trust God to guide your financial journey, and remember that His wisdom, not our wealth, is our greatest treasure.

Proverbs 3:9-10 says, *"Honor the Lord with your wealth, with the firstfruits of all your crops; then your barns will be filled to overflowing, and your vats will brim over with new wine."* As we honor God with our investments, He promises to bless us abundantly, enabling us to live generously and fulfill His calling on our lives.

In the end, investing isn't about making money; it's about making an impact. It's about honoring God with our resources, creating a legacy, and using wealth as a tool to serve others. So start today, invest with purpose, and watch as God multiplies what you have for His glory.

Discussion Questions:

1. What history does your family have with investing?

2. Risk tolerance is your ability to absorb fluctuations in the market that have a negative impact on your investments. How do you mitigate some of the risk of investing?

3. How does leverage (borrowing) affect your ability to invest? What are the risks, challenges and rewards using debt to finance an investment?

4. Retirement isn't discussed in the Bible. What are some biblical goals of investing? How do they differ from a Retirement focus?

9
MAKING BIBLICAL ECONOMICS WORK IN YOUR LIFE

"Honor the Lord with your wealth, with the firstfruits of all your crops; then your barns will be filled to overflowing, and your vats will brim over with new wine."

— Proverbs 3:9-10 (NIV)

For most of my life, I thought finances were simply about making money, saving, and making sure I could cover my bills. But over the years, I've come to see that the Bible speaks about money in a way that's deeply integrated with our faith. Finances are not just a practical part of life but a spiritual discipline. When we manage money biblically, we're not just stewarding our resources; we're walking in obedience and opening ourselves to God's blessings.

Managing money isn't just a worldly skill; it's a spiritual act of worship. I've seen it firsthand in my own life and in the lives of others: when we put God at the center of our finances, everything changes. Proverbs 3:9-10 teaches that when we honor God with our wealth, He responds with abundance—not always in the ways we expect, but always in ways that enrich our lives. Let's dig into what it looks like to apply biblical principles to your finances, especially if you're starting out.

1. Tithing and Trusting

When we give our first fruits, we're declaring that God is the source of our provision. Tithing is one of the most tangible ways to put God first in our finances. Malachi 3:10 says, *"Bring the whole tithe into the storehouse, that there may be food in my house. Test me in this, says the Lord Almighty, and see if I will not throw open the floodgates of heaven and pour out so much blessing that there will not be room enough to store it."* This promise holds a unique place in Scripture—it's the only place where God invites us to test Him.

For many, tithing feels counterintuitive, especially if finances are tight. I remember when I first started tithing consistently. It felt like a leap of faith, but as I gave that first 10%, God provided in ways I couldn't have imagined. Tithing isn't about the amount; it's about the heart. It's a way to demonstrate our trust in God, declaring that we believe He can do more with 90% than we could ever do with 100%.

2. Living Below Your Means

One of the most important principles in biblical economics is contentment. Hebrews 13:5 tells us, *"Keep your lives free from the love of money and be content with what you have, because God has said, 'Never will I leave you; never will I forsake you.'"* Contentment doesn't mean we can't have nice things; it means our identity and happiness aren't tied to material possessions.

Living below your means is a practical way to exercise contentment. It's easy to fall into the trap of upgrading our lifestyle with every raise or bonus, but biblical wisdom calls us to save and give generously instead. When we live simply, we find that we actually have more freedom—not less. Money saved can go toward emergencies, investments, or helping others, all of which bring a lasting sense of joy and purpose.

Practical Steps to Living Below Your Means

1. **Budget for Essentials First** – Start by budgeting for your needs: housing, food, transportation, and healthcare. Knowing your true essentials will help you avoid unnecessary spending.
2. **Save for Large Purchases** – Avoid debt by saving for big-ticket items. Proverbs 21:20 says, *"The wise store up choice food and olive oil, but fools gulp theirs down."* Wise people plan ahead, while impulsive spending often leads to regret.
3. **Distinguish Between Wants and Needs** – Not everything we desire is essential. Practice asking, "Is this necessary?" If it's a want, give yourself time to consider the purchase instead of buying immediately.

3. Investing Wisely with God's Guidance

The Bible doesn't just encourage saving; it also speaks to the importance of investing wisely. Proverbs 21:5 teaches, *"The plans of the diligent lead to profit as surely as haste leads to poverty."* Investing is about growing what God has given us, so we can increase our ability to provide, bless others, and support God's work.

But investing isn't gambling—it's a planned, educated decision. Before you invest, make sure you're educated on what you're investing in. Seek God's wisdom and surround yourself with knowledgeable advisors. Not every investment is right for every person, so be prayerful and diligent in choosing investments that align with your goals and values.

4. Embracing Generosity

One of the most beautiful aspects of biblical economics is the emphasis on generosity. Acts 20:35 says, *"It is more blessed to give than to receive."* Generosity reflects the heart of God, and when we give, we're participating in His Kingdom work.

Generosity doesn't always mean financial giving; it can include your time, talents, and resources. When you give, whether to your church, a charity, or someone in need, you're storing up treasures in heaven. It may seem like a sacrifice at the moment, but God's blessings often follow our acts of generosity. He's faithful to replenish what we give, sometimes financially, but always in ways that deepen our faith and joy.

5. Planning for the Future

As Christians, we're called to be forward-thinking with our finances. Proverbs 6:6-8 encourages us to observe the ant, which stores up provisions in the summer to prepare for the winter. Planning for the future isn't a lack of faith; it's wise stewardship.

Setting Goals and Developing a Financial Plan

When planning for the future, start by setting clear financial goals. Maybe you want to save for a house, start a business, or ensure a comfortable retirement. Write down your goals, pray over them, and ask God for guidance. Then, create a plan that includes saving, investing, and giving.

1. **Set Short and Long-Term Goals** – Start with small, attainable goals and build up to bigger ones.

2. **Review and Adjust Your Plan** – Life changes, and so will your goals and financial needs. Review your plan regularly and adjust as necessary.

3. **Trust God's Timing** – Financial planning requires patience. Trust that as you work diligently, God will provide in His time.

6. Avoiding Debt as a Lifestyle

Debt can be a financial burden that distracts us from God's work. Proverbs 22:7 warns, *"The borrower is slave to the lender."* While debt is sometimes necessary for larger purchases, like a home, God's wisdom encourages us to avoid unnecessary debt whenever possible. When we're not weighed down by debt, we're free to follow God's call without financial constraints.

Strategies to Manage and Avoid Debt

1. **Pay with Cash** – Using cash or a debit card can help curb spending, as it's easier to track and control.

2. **Avoid Credit Card Debt** – Credit cards often carry high-interest rates, which can spiral into significant debt if not managed carefully. Try to pay your balance in full each month.

3. **Develop a Debt-Repayment Plan** – If you have debt, create a plan to pay it off as soon as possible. Start with the smallest debts and work your way up, gaining momentum as you go.

7. Trusting God's Provision

Ultimately, applying biblical economics means trusting that God will provide for all our needs. Philippians 4:19 reminds us, *"And my God will meet all your needs according to the riches of his glory in Christ Jesus."* Our financial journey may have ups and downs, but we can rest assured that God's provision is constant.

Cultivating Gratitude

A heart of gratitude transforms the way we see our finances. When we're grateful, we're less likely to focus on what we lack and more inclined to see God's blessings in our lives. Gratitude opens the door to contentment, peace, and joy, regardless of our financial situation.

1. **Reflect on God's Past Provision** – Keep a journal of answered prayers and blessings. Looking back can strengthen your faith in God's future provision.

2. **Thank God Daily** – Make gratitude a daily habit. Thank Him not just for financial blessings, but for all the ways He cares for you.
3. **Celebrate Small Victories** – Recognize and celebrate progress, even small wins. Each step forward is a reminder of God's faithfulness.

Biblical economics isn't about rigid rules or a prosperity gospel; it's about aligning our financial decisions with God's principles. When we handle our money in a way that honors Him, we experience financial freedom, peace, and a deeper relationship with our Creator. Applying these principles may not make us wealthy by the world's standards, but it positions us for a life of purpose, impact, and lasting joy.

Remember, God is the ultimate provider. As we commit our finances to Him, let's walk forward in faith, trusting that His wisdom and love will guide us every step of the way.

Discussion Questions:

1. What does it mean to you to trust God with your money?

2. What next steps will you take to trust him more?

3. How have the things you have learned in this course so far changed your financial life?

4. How can you deal with the pressure from others to live above your means?

10
MANAGING FOR ETERNITY – BUILDING WEALTH THAT LASTS FOREVER

"Do not store up for yourselves treasures on earth, where moths and vermin destroy, and where thieves break in and steal. But store up for yourselves treasures in heaven."

— Matthew 6:19-20 (NIV)

When I started out, financial independence meant reaching a point where I didn't have to worry about money. But as I grew in my walk with God, I realized that true financial success means more than personal freedom or comfort; it's about stewarding wealth for a purpose that lasts beyond this life. Jesus taught us that material wealth can be fleeting, but what we do with our resources has the power to impact eternity.

In a world that tells us to seek more for ourselves, managing our finances with an eternal mindset challenges us to live differently. We aren't here to build temporary empires; we're here to build God's Kingdom. Managing for eternity means looking at our money through the lens of eternity and aligning our financial goals with God's purposes. Let's look at what it means to manage our resources with a Kingdom perspective, because this approach is both a privilege and a responsibility.

1. Understanding Earthly Wealth and Heavenly Treasures

One of the core messages of the Bible is that wealth, in itself, isn't wrong; it's how we use it that counts. Matthew 6:19-21 tells us to store up treasures in heaven rather than on earth. This doesn't mean that saving or investing is unwise, but it challenges us to examine where our ultimate focus lies. Are we more invested in material wealth or in eternal impact?

The Apostle Paul reminds us in 1 Timothy 6:17-19, *"Command those who are rich in this present world not to be arrogant nor to put their hope in wealth, which is so uncertain, but to put their hope in God, who richly provides us with everything for our enjoyment."* Wealth is a gift, a resource we're called to manage wisely, but it's not where our security or identity should lie. When our hope is anchored in God, we're freed from the pressure of chasing after worldly wealth and can focus on stewarding it for eternal good.

Earthly Wealth as a Tool, Not a Goal

God doesn't measure success by the balance in our bank account; He looks at how we use what He's given us. Financial success for a Christian isn't about accumulation but about distribution—using our resources to make an impact. When we view earthly wealth as a tool, we start to see opportunities to invest in things that matter eternally: helping those in need, supporting ministry, and building a legacy of faith.

2. Aligning Financial Goals with Kingdom Values

One of the most powerful ways to live with an eternal mindset is to align our financial goals with God's priorities. Proverbs 3:9-10 says, *"Honor the Lord with your wealth, with the firstfruits of all your crops; then your barns will be filled to overflowing."* When we prioritize God in our finances, He blesses us—not always with more money, but with a sense of purpose and peace that money can't buy.

When I began to focus on Kingdom values in my finances, it changed everything. I started setting aside a portion of my income specifically for giving. I no longer saw it as a "loss" but as an investment in eternity. Whether it was supporting my church, helping a friend in need, or giving to missions, I found joy in knowing that my money was doing something meaningful.

Practical Steps to Align Your Finances with Kingdom Values

1. **Budget for Generosity** – Make giving a line item in your budget. By setting aside a portion of your income each month for generosity, you're reminding yourself that God is the ultimate provider.

2. **Set Kingdom-Oriented Financial Goals** – Instead of just saving for retirement or a new car, set goals that reflect your faith. Consider goals like funding a mission trip, supporting a ministry, or building an emergency fund for unexpected needs in your community.

3. **Pray Over Your Finances** – Ask God to guide you in making financial decisions that honor Him. James 1:5 tells us, *"If any of you lacks wisdom, let him ask of God, who gives to all liberally and without reproach, and it will be given to him."* When we seek God's wisdom, He helps us make choices that are in line with His purposes.

3. Cultivating Contentment in a World of More

One of the greatest challenges of managing for eternity is cultivating contentment in a culture that constantly pushes for more. We're bombarded daily with messages telling us that we need the latest gadgets, a bigger house, or a newer car. But the Bible calls us to a different standard. Hebrews 13:5 says, *"Keep your lives free from the love of money and be content with what you have."*

Contentment isn't about settling for less; it's about recognizing that we have enough because God provides for us. When we're content, we're able to give freely and joyfully. We no longer feel the need to hoard or compare ourselves to others. Instead, we're focused on what we can give, not just what we can get.

Practical Ways to Practice Contentment

1. **Limit Impulse Buying** – Give yourself time to consider if a purchase is truly necessary or if it's just a response to a fleeting desire.

2. **Practice Gratitude Daily** – Make a habit of thanking God for the blessings you already have. Gratitude shifts our focus from what we lack to what we have, fostering a sense of abundance rather than scarcity.

3. **Find Fulfillment in Eternal Investments** – Instead of seeking happiness in material possessions, find fulfillment in things that last. Relationships, serving others, and building your faith all bring joy that material things can't match.

4. Building a Legacy That Lasts Beyond This Life

Psalm 78:4 reminds us to *"tell the next generation the praiseworthy deeds of the Lord, his power, and the wonders he has done."* Managing our finances with eternity in mind means building a legacy of faith, generosity, and stewardship. This legacy isn't just about leaving money for future generations; it's about instilling values that will guide them.

One of the best ways to build this legacy is by modeling financial faithfulness. When those around us see us living with an eternal perspective—choosing generosity over greed, contentment over consumerism—they're impacted by our example. Whether it's our children, friends, or community, our choices inspire others to live with a Kingdom mindset.

Practical Steps for Building an Eternal Legacy

1. **Teach Generosity** – If you have children or young people in your life, involve them in your giving. Let them see the joy that comes from blessing others.

2. **Write Down Your Values** – Document your beliefs and values regarding money and stewardship. This becomes a guide for future generations and a reminder of what mattered most to you.

3. **Invest in People** – Money isn't the only way to leave a legacy. Investing time, sharing wisdom, and mentoring others are all ways to build a legacy that lasts.

5. Living with an Eternal Perspective Every Day

Romans 12:2 tells us, *"Do not conform to the pattern of this world, but be transformed by the renewing of your mind."* Living with an eternal perspective requires us to renew our minds daily, reminding ourselves that our true home is in heaven, not on earth. Each financial decision, big or small, becomes an opportunity to reflect our faith and values.

This perspective doesn't mean we never buy anything nice or enjoy the fruits of our labor. It means that even in our enjoyment, we're aware of the bigger picture. We see our resources as gifts from God, entrusted to us to manage for His glory.

Daily Habits for an Eternal Mindset

1. **Pray Over Major Financial Decisions** – Before making significant purchases or investments, seek God's guidance. Invite Him into your decisions and ask Him to direct your path.

2. **Regularly Assess Your Financial Goals** – Periodically review your financial goals to ensure they align with Kingdom values. Are you still focused on generosity? Are your priorities in line with God's calling for your life?

3. **Remember That God Is Your Provider** – Trusting that God will meet our needs frees us from the fear of scarcity. Matthew 6:33 reminds us, *"Seek first his kingdom and his righteousness, and all these things will be given to you as well."* When we seek God's Kingdom first, we can trust Him to take care of everything else.

Living with eternity in mind transforms the way we manage money. It shifts our focus from building personal wealth to building God's Kingdom. When we choose to live this way, our finances become a powerful testimony of faith. Every dollar spent, saved, or given is an opportunity to honor God and invest in something that will last forever. This is the kind of wealth that truly matters, the kind that brings peace, joy, and purpose. By managing for eternity, we're not just securing our own future—we're impacting lives, supporting God's work, and leaving a legacy that will echo into eternity.

Discussion Questions:

1. What are the top three things you are going to do to align your financial life with God's purpose for your life?

2. What are you thankful for?

3. What does it mean to be a steward of the resources that you have been trusted with?

Example 1:

Budget vs Actual

Month ______________________________

	Budget	Actual	Variance
Savings & Investing			
Emergency Fund	1,000.00	1,000.00	
Future Expenses			
Retirement Fund	1,500.00	1,650.00	
Total Savings & Investing	2,500.00	2,650.00	(150.00)
Housing			
Rent/Mortgage	3,500.00	3,500.00	
Insurance			
Taxes			
Maintenance		250.00	
Other			
Total Housing	3,500.00	3,750.00	(250.00)
Transportation			
Car debt	-		
Fuel	300.00	275.00	

Maintenance (Oil Changes/Repairs)			
Insurance	560.00	560.00	
License/Registration		75.00	
Total Transportation	860.00	910.00	(50.00)

Utilities

Gas	2,000.00	1,875.00	
Electric			
Water			
Trash			
Telephone			
Cable/Internet			
Total Utilities	2,000.00	1,875.00	125.00

Food

Groceries	400.00	415.00	
Take Out	400.00	480.00	
Snacks			
Total Food	800.00	895.00	(95.00)

Entertainment

Restaraunts	200.00	400.00	
Vacations	250.00	500.00	

Other			
Total Entertainment	450.00	900.00	(450.00)
Donations			
Church	2,000.00	2,000.00	
Other			
Total Donations	2,000.00	2,000.00	-
Total Expenses	12,110.00	12,980.00	(870.00)
Net Take Home Income	12,110.00	13,500.00	(1,390.00)
Surplus*/(Deficit)	-	520.00	(520.00)

* Surplus adds to savings, while deficits will deduct from savings

Example 2:

The Cost of Waiting to Invest

	Bill		8.00%	
Year	Investment	New Balance	Return	Balance
20	1,200.00	1,200.00	96.00	1,296.00
21	1,200.00	2,496.00	199.68	2,695.68
22	1,200.00	3,895.68	311.65	4,207.33
23	1,200.00	5,407.33	432.59	5,839.92
24	1,200.00	7,039.92	563.19	7,603.11
25	1,200.00	8,803.11	704.25	9,507.36
26	1,200.00	10,707.36	856.59	11,563.95
27	1,200.00	12,763.95	1,021.12	13,785.07
28	1,200.00	14,985.07	1,198.81	16,183.87
29	1,200.00	17,383.87	1,390.71	18,774.58
30	,200.00	19,974.58	1,597.97	21,572.55
31		21,572.55	1,725.80	23,298.36
32		23,298.36	1,863.87	25,162.22
33		25,162.22	2,012.98	27,175.20
34		27,175.20	2,174.02	29,349.22
35		29,349.22	2,347.94	31,697.16
36		31,697.16	2,535.77	34,232.93
37		34,232.93	2,738.63	36,971.56
38		36,971.56	2,957.73	39,929.29
39		39,929.29	3,194.34	43,123.63
40		43,123.63	3,449.89	46,573.52
41		46,573.52	3,725.88	50,299.40
42		50,299.40	4,023.95	54,323.36
43		54,323.36	4,345.87	58,669.22
44		58,669.22	4,693.54	63,362.76
45		63,362.76	5,069.02	68,431.78
46		68,431.78	5,474.54	73,906.32

47	73,906.32	5,912.51	79,818.83
48	79,818.83	6,385.51	86,204.34
49	86,204.34	6,896.35	93,100.68
50	93,100.68	7,448.05	100,548.74
51	100,548.74	8,043.90	108,592.64
52	108,592.64	8,687.41	117,280.05
53	117,280.05	9,382.40	126,662.45
54	126,662.45	10,133.00	136,795.45
55	136,795.45	10,943.64	147,739.09
56	147,739.09	11,819.13	159,558.21
57	159,558.21	12,764.66	172,322.87
58	172,322.87	13,785.83	186,108.70
59	186,108.70	14,888.70	200,997.39
60	200,997.39	16,079.79	217,077.19
61	217,077.19	17,366.17	234,443.36
62	234,443.36	18,755.47	253,198.83
63	253,198.83	20,255.91	273,454.74
64	273,454.74	21,876.38	295,331.12
65	295,331.12	23,626.49	318,957.60

13,200.00	305,757.60

	TOM		8.00%	
Year	**Investment**	**New Balance**	**Return**	**Balance**
20	-	-	-	-
21	-	-	-	-
22	-	-	-	-
23	-	-	-	-
24	-	-	-	-
25	-	-	-	-
26	-	-	-	-
27	-	-	-	-
28	-	-	-	-
29	-	-	-	-
30	-	-	-	-
31	1,200.00	1,200.00	96.00	1,296.00
32	1,200.00	2,496.00	199.68	2,695.68
33	1,200.00	3,895.68	311.65	4,207.33
34	1,200.00	5,407.33	432.59	5,839.92
35	1,200.00	7,039.92	563.19	7,603.11
36	1,200.00	8,803.11	704.25	9,507.36
37	1,200.00	10,707.36	856.59	11,563.95
38	1,200.00	12,763.95	1,021.12	13,785.07
39	1,200.00	14,985.07	1,198.81	16,183.87
40	1,200.00	17,383.87	1,390.71	18,774.58
41	1,200.00	19,974.58	1,597.97	21,572.55
42	1,200.00	22,772.55	1,821.80	24,594.36
43	1,200.00	25,794.36	2,063.55	27,857.90
44	1,200.00	29,057.90	2,324.63	31,382.54
45	1,200.00	32,582.54	2,606.60	35,189.14
46	1,200.00	36,389.14	2,911.13	39,300.27
47	1,200.00	40,500.27	3,240.02	43,740.29
48	1,200.00	44,940.29	3,595.22	48,535.52
49	1,200.00	49,735.52	3,978.84	53,714.36
50	1,200.00	54,914.36	4,393.15	59,307.51
51	1,200.00	60,507.51	4,840.60	65,348.11
52	1,200.00	66,548.11	5,323.85	71,871.95

53	1,200.00	73,071.95	5,845.76	78,917.71
54	1,200.00	80,117.71	6,409.42	86,527.13
55	1,200.00	87,727.13	7,018.17	94,745.30
56	1,200.00	95,945.30	7,675.62	103,620.92
57	1,200.00	104,820.92	8,385.67	113,206.60
58	1,200.00	114,406.60	9,152.53	123,559.12
59	1,200.00	124,759.12	9,980.73	134,739.85
60	1,200.00	135,939.85	10,875.19	146,815.04
61	1,200.00	148,015.04	11,841.20	159,856.24
62	1,200.00	161,056.24	12,884.50	173,940.74
63	1,200.00	175,140.74	14,011.26	189,152.00
64	1,200.00	190,352.00	15,228.16	205,580.16
65	1,200.00	206,780.16	16,542.41	223,322.58
	42,000.00		181,322.58	

	DAVE		8.00%	
Year	**Investment**	**New Balance**	**Return**	**Balance**
20	1,200.00	1,200.00	96.00	1,296.00
21	1,200.00	2,496.00	199.68	2,695.68
22	1,200.00	3,895.68	311.65	4,207.33
23	1,200.00	5,407.33	432.59	5,839.92
24	1,200.00	7,039.92	563.19	7,603.11
25	1,200.00	8,803.11	704.25	9,507.36
26	1,200.00	10,707.36	856.59	11,563.95
27	1,200.00	12,763.95	1,021.12	13,785.07
28	1,200.00	14,985.07	1,198.81	16,183.87
29	1,200.00	17,383.87	1,390.71	18,774.58
30	1,200.00	19,974.58	1,597.97	21,572.55
31	1,200.00	22,772.55	1,821.80	24,594.36
32	1,200.00	25,794.36	2,063.55	27,857.90
33	1,200.00	29,057.90	2,324.63	31,382.54
34	1,200.00	32,582.54	2,606.60	35,189.14
35	1,200.00	36,389.14	2,911.13	39,300.27
36	1,200.00	40,500.27	3,240.02	43,740.29
37	1,200.00	44,940.29	3,595.22	48,535.52
38	1,200.00	49,735.52	3,978.84	53,714.36
39	1,200.00	54,914.36	4,393.15	59,307.51
40	1,200.00	60,507.51	4,840.60	65,348.11
41	1,200.00	66,548.11	5,323.85	71,871.95
42	1,200.00	73,071.95	5,845.76	78,917.71
43	1,200.00	80,117.71	6,409.42	86,527.13
44	1,200.00	87,727.13	7,018.17	94,745.30
45	1,200.00	95,945.30	7,675.62	103,620.92
46	1,200.00	104,820.92	8,385.67	113,206.60
47	1,200.00	114,406.60	9,152.53	123,559.12
48	1,200.00	124,759.12	9,980.73	134,739.85
49	1,200.00	135,939.85	10,875.19	146,815.04
50	1,200.00	148,015.04	11,841.20	159,856.24
51	1,200.00	161,056.24	12,884.50	173,940.74
52	1,200.00	175,140.74	14,011.26	189,152.00

53	1,200.00	190,352.00	15,228.16	205,580.16
54	1,200.00	206,780.16	16,542.41	223,322.58
55	1,200.00	224,522.58	17,961.81	242,484.38
56	1,200.00	243,684.38	19,494.75	263,179.13
57	1,200.00	264,379.13	21,150.33	285,529.47
58	1,200.00	286,729.47	22,938.36	309,667.82
59	1,200.00	310,867.82	24,869.43	335,737.25
60	1,200.00	336,937.25	26,954.98	363,892.23
61	1,200.00	365,092.23	29,207.38	394,299.61
62	1,200.00	395,499.61	31,639.97	427,139.57
63	1,200.00	428,339.57	34,267.17	462,606.74
64	1,200.00	463,806.74	37,104.54	500,911.28
65	1,200.00	502,111.28	40,168.90	542,280.18
	55,200.00		487,080.18	

About the Author

Brandon Moore is a CPA, Certified Wealth Strategist©, coach, and real estate investor who has successfully purchased and managed more than one hundred residences—while equipping others to thrive in reaching their financial goals. Like many successful entrepreneurs, however, Brandon's career path hasn't been direct. The curves in his route have defined his success—while deepening his expertise.

Brandon graduated from Angelo State University in San Angelo, Texas and began investing in real estate. A few years later, he acquired his CPA designation, and at age thirty-one, bought his first CPA firm—while building his real estate empire. Later, he purchased another four accounting practices. And during the 2008 recession, he acquired his financial service licenses to better serve CPA clients.

Today, Brandon advises clients on wealth management, retirement planning, and faithful stewardship of what God's provision. Brandon and his wife of twenty-nine years, Angela, invest in and manage single-family properties and duplexes. They have four awesome children, two wonderful daughter-in-loves, one fantastic son-in-love, and one amazing grandchild.

Brandon believes his purpose is to help churches, leaders, and individuals find their way forward to grow within themselves and the organizations they serve.

In his free time, Brandon loves art, music and plays multiple instruments. Brandon usually has two or three art projects going at once. You can see his portfolio at www.brandonsartlife.com. Brandon also reached his goal of third-degree black belt in Taekwondo, believing that martial arts offer a continuous improvement philosophy—training both mind and body.

Connect with Brandon at www.brandonkmoore.com.

Made in the USA
Monee, IL
05 November 2026

67374708R00050